THE ULTIMATE PATH TO FORGIVENESS

Unlocking Your Power

Book 1

KATHARINE C. GIOVANNI

Copyright 2023 by Katharine C. Giovanni
The Ultimate Path To Forgiveness
Unlocking Your Power
Published by:
NewRoad Publishing
A Giowell Group LLC Company
Telephone: 919-263-4003
Email: ron@giowellgroup.com.

First Edition 2023
An application to register this book for cataloging has been submitted to the Library of Congress.

Paperback ISBN: 978-1-931109-26-0
eBook ISBN: 978-1-931109-27-7

Printed in the United States of America

Cover Design by Angie Alaya

DISCLAIMERS AND LEGAL NOTICES

The information provided in this book is designed to provide helpful information on the subjects discussed. This book is not meant to be used, nor should it be used, to diagnose or treat any medical condition. For diagnosis or treatment of any medical problem, please consult your physician. The author and NewRoad Publishing are not responsible for any specific health needs that may require medical supervision and are not liable for any damages or negative consequences from any treatment, action, application or preparation to any person reading or following the information in this book. References are provided for informational purposes only and do not constitute endorsement of any websites or sources. Readers should be aware that the websites in this book may change.

Information Accuracy

The author and NewRoad Publishing make every effort to ensure that all information presented in this book is correct. However, we do not guarantee the accuracy of the information contained in this book, and reliance on information provided in this book is solely at your own risk. Every effort has been made to make this book as complete as possible; however, it may yet contain mistakes, both typographical and substantive. Therefore, this book should be used only as a general guide.

Disclaimer of Warranties

This book is provided solely on an "as-is" basis, and the use of the information contained herein is at your sole risk. Except to the extent required by any mandatory applicable law, this book and the information contained herein are not subject to any warranty or condition, express or implied, including, without limitation, any warranty of merchantability, satisfactory quality, fitness for a particular purpose or use, or non-infringement.

Neither the author nor NewRoad Publishing guarantees the accuracy or completeness of any information contained in this book. Neither the author nor NewRoad Publishing assumes any liability or responsibility for any errors or omissions in the information contained in the book. Neither the author nor NewRoad Publishing makes any representations or warranties of any kind, express or implied, as to the book or the information contained herein or the results that may be obtained from the use of information contained in the book. The book and the information contained therein are not, and should not be considered to be, presenting you with any type of business opportunity offering or its equivalent.

Limitation of Liability

Neither the author nor NewRoad Publishing shall be liable for any damages of any kind arising from or in connection with the use of the book or the information contained therein, including, without limitation, mistakes, omissions, errors, or defects, even if the author or NewRoad Publishing is expressly advised of the possibility of such damages. This is a comprehensive limitation of liability that applies to all damages of any kind, including compensatory, direct, indirect, punitive, special, incidental or consequential damages (including but not limited to damages for lost profits or loss of revenue.

OTHER BOOKS

BY KATHARINE GIOVANNI

- The Ultimate Path To Forgiveness
- The Little Bird on Your Shoulder
- Rainbows and Banana Peels
- The Concierge Manual
- Going Above and Beyond
- God, Is That You?
- 101 Great Ways to Improve Your Life: Volume 3, Contributing Author)
- Inspiring Hope, (Contributing Author)

ACKNOWLEDGMENTS

I want to give a huge shoutout to the incredible people who helped me while I wrote this book.

My husband, Ron, and our two amazing sons. Your unwavering support, love, wisdom, and assistance were absolutely invaluable. I couldn't have done it without you guys by my side, keeping me motivated and cheering me on.

My incredible soul sisters and earth angels Katie Nall, Ph.D., and Paula Dice. Thank you for gracing me with your friendship, your boundless wisdom, and your endless patience with me.

I am so grateful and blessed to have all of you in my life. You are the true superheroes of this book.

The five of you hold a special place in my heart, and you mean the entire universe to me.

Katharine

TABLE OF CONTENTS

FOREWORD

By Katie Nall, Ph.D.

"Don't ever underestimate the power of forgiveness. I've seen it free people. I've seen it lift burdens that had weighed them down and kept them from moving on."

Buffy Andrews

I forgive you.

Such sweet words to hear.

And yet those same words sometimes get stuck in my throat.

I've read the self-help books and understand the process of forgiving is for my benefit rather than for my offender.

Somehow saying the words, "I forgive you," doesn't seem enough. The words alone don't seem sufficient. The phrase was what mothers all over the world insisted their children repeat to annoying siblings and hurtful friends.

And when I repeated those words in my childhood as directed, somehow, I never felt the peace Katharine talks about in her book.

As an adult, the memory of the lost effect of repeating "I forgive you" in my childhood kept me from exercising my right to forgive. The words alone felt hollow.

Katharine's book, "The Ultimate Path to Forgiveness," provides step-by-step instructions beyond just repeating the empty phrase learned in my childhood.

Her decades of research and practice teaching her techniques provide not only background, but also the foundation of the book. Personal experience and unusual reactions after completing her Forgiveness Matrix™ Emphasize the effectiveness of her technique especially as she introduces different facets of forgiveness. She asks us to journey with her as she discovers the various levels of pain and how to address each level. And by the end of the book, you can feel the release of pent-up hurt.

And if you don't read her book and try her techniques, well, know that I forgive you.

And because I used "The Ultimate Path to Forgiveness," I mean it this time.

Katie Nall, Ph.D.

Vero Beach, FL

October 2023

CHAPTER 1

"Forgive others, not because they deserve forgiveness but because you deserve peace."

Jonathan Lockwood Huie

I have a confession. It took me a long time to forgive the people in my past. It wasn't because I couldn't. Quite frankly, it was because I simply didn't want to. I wanted to stay angry.

I was too committed to "my story" to give it up. It had become my identity.

My new normal, so to speak.

Besides, if I didn't have "my story," then who exactly would I be? It was too scary a thought to even consider.

My story featured a heroine who was a survivor of an alcoholic family. From family drama and divorce to health issues and money trouble, it was all there.

I was a survivor, I used to tell myself, and I happily wallowed in that for years.

As time went on, long-held resentments frequently drifted to the front of my mind, and I often got lost in the memories.

I was negative all the time, angry at the world in general, and completely miserable. I honestly had no idea how to get out of the hell that I was in.

I could have changed my life, but it was easier to stay the way I was - angry, unhealthy, and emotionally poor.

It was familiar. I was used to it. The devil you know is better than the devil you don't, right? I knew where all the potholes in the road were and got used to stepping around them.

Until I couldn't.

It wasn't until I hit my late thirties that I finally began to understand my anger was holding me back and the resentments were making me sick.

Literally.

I had stomach issues, got colds and the flu easily, and often felt poorly. Money was an issue all the time, and my stress level was high.

Something had to give.

I changed when I finally realized that I needed to lose the story and forgive people for **ME**.

I wanted to stop thinking about my persecutors all the time!

I didn't want a relationship with those who hurt me; I wanted to be permanently free of them. They had taken up enough space in my mind and had been living there rent free for too long.

It was time to evict them.

So I began researching forgiveness.

Not surprisingly, I discovered the gift of forgiveness can be found in every religion around the world.

For example, when Jesus was asked how many times we should forgive someone, he replied by saying we should forgive others "seventy times seven."

In Buddhism, forgiveness is "seen as a practice to prevent harmful emotions from causing havoc on one's mental well-being." Buddhism also recognizes feelings of hatred and ill-will leave a lasting effect on our mind.

Lastly, In Judaism, forgiveness is considered a pious act.

I read books and articles on the topic, went to workshops, and eventually did my best to forgive all the haters in my life. While I was unable to completely forgive some of these people as just the appearance of their name would often set me off, I kept doing it anyways.

What I finally came to understand was forgiveness is a journey.

It's a long staircase with several levels. The trick is to keep climbing and not stay too long on each landing because if you do, you risk slipping back down into the basement again.

You know which basement. The dark and scary one filled with anger and resentment.

The interesting effect of forgiveness is once you completely and totally forgive, you can't easily recall the details of those bad memories. Instead, you remember the good memories.

Please don't get me wrong, I can easily dredge up bad memories and start wallowing in them again. I don't because doing so will make me sick, angry, and resentful again: feelings I don't want or need anymore. I prefer joy, happiness, and love.

You may be asking yourself: What if you didn't HAVE any good memories with this hater?

After completing the Forgiveness Matrix™ you will stop focusing on those haters, the incidents, and more importantly, the pain. Plus, if you see your perpetrators' name you'll likely stare at it with no emotion and move on.

When the haters' names no longer affect you is when you know you've completely forgiven them! You can see their name with no negative emotion. Actually, you won't have any emotion at all, good or bad. Their name will simply be a name on a page.

Remember, forgiving someone does **<u>NOT</u>** mean they were right. It simply means you are sick and tired of being angry, sick, and tired.

It means that you just want to move on.

CHAPTER 2

"Holding on to anger is like grasping a hot coal with the intent of throwing it at someone else; you are the one who gets burned."

Buddha

I began teaching people how to start a concierge/ lifestyle management business in 1999 which included how to offer over-the-top concierge-level customer service.

Put simply, I taught them how to be nice to people. Being super friendly and nice to people who you don't actually like is one of the keys to being a great concierge.

As the leader and one of the original founders of the independent concierge industry, it was my responsibility to be an example of five-star concierge-level customer service. How could I teach concierges how to be to be nice if I didn't practice the principles myself?

4

Over the years, I led workshops and trained thousands of concierges world-wide. Part of the training was to teach concierge and front-line staff how to maintain a warm, friendly, and positive attitude regardless of the situation.

It's seriously hard for a concierge to keep a positive and upbeat attitude when they feel anger, frustration, or embarrassment because the last guest/resident was rude, nasty, or just plain acting ugly.

What if you're angry at someone from your personal life? Hiding that anger is even harder. You lose your focus because your anger is all you can think about. Not to mention the number of times you talk about your personal anger to your co-workers.

I can teach you how to say the most beautiful words in the world, with the most pleasing tone of voice, and it won't matter at all if you are angry. Because your anger will bleed through your body language whether you want it to or not - unless you have trained acting skills and can alter your body language, a skill only a few people have.

Around 2002, I remember leaning back in my chair and staring at my computer wondering how I could help my students recover from a disruptive encounter and be their best for the next guest/resident? The real trick was they had to be able to recover quickly because they probably wouldn't be able to leave their workstation. I also wondered how I could get rid of their anger - not just for one shift, but permanently.

The act of forgiveness came to my mind. I had been practicing a simple form of forgiveness since my mother died in 1990. It helped mitigate some of my anger.

Could I apply forgiveness to a business workshop?

In those days, the mere thought of introducing a "soft" topic like forgiveness during business sessions was unheard of, and even considered taboo. Despite the unpopularity of teaching forgiveness, the idea lingered in my mind.

I decided to use myself as a guinea pig before offering the topic of forgiveness to my students. A friend of mine suggested I write a list of my personal haters. One night I wrote a list of the people I thought I should forgive. Then I slowly went through the list and forgave each one before I went to bed.

I started by forgiving someone who I thought would be easy to forgive. As I stared at that person's name, my mind automatically went back in time to when I had a fight with them. They were an old friend of mine from school who I hadn't spoken with in years. It was easy to forgive them, especially since I couldn't remember what we fought about so long ago!

I got a clear picture of them in my mind. Then I placed my hand on my heart, I forgave them, and I really meant it. My hand served as a reminder to say the words from my heart. No mantra. No crystals. No incense. Just three simple words "I forgive you." I knew it worked because I could actually feel energy subtly leave my chest.

About two hours later, that same old friend called me! Remember, we hadn't spoken in decades. The conversation went well, and we caught up with one another's lives. Curiously, I asked my old friend why they called me today after all these years.

Their answer nearly made me fall off my chair.

Apparently two hours prior, exactly when I was forgiving them, a small figurine I gave them in school randomly fell off their shelf onto the floor. As they picked it up, they decided to call me.

WOW! That is some powerful energy we're talking about! These events happened while we were over 700 miles away from each other.

Over the next few months I intentionally forgave all kinds of people – from the bullies in elementary school, to loved ones who caused me pain. I started with the least painful memories, like my friends from grammar school, and saved the most painful ones for last.

The most painful ones? I simply forgave them and moved on. Sometimes you have to walk around a wall to move on. So I decided to just circle back sometime in the future and try again.

Did I ever finally forgive them? Yes. Years later when I did the Forgiveness Matrix™ in this book.

I learned that by forgiving people, my work and relationships improved dramatically. Honestly, the process of forgiving has been fantastic. Plus I began to feel better.

I also learned something REALLY interesting.

When I started to forgive people in my personal life, my company sales went up.

WHAT?

Forgiveness and money are tied together?

I was stunned when I discovered the relationship.

I learned that un-forgiveness stops all sorts of positive things from happening in your life. Money, career, health, happiness, relationships... all are affected by forgiveness, or the lack of it.

Magical things happen when you forgive!

After my personal experiences with forgiveness techniques, I began adding the topic to my workshops.

It's been over 20 years since I first researched and applied forgiveness, and I have taught thousands of people worldwide about the power of forgiveness.

Interestingly, I noticed a recurring phenomenon: one or two students had to leave the room during the forgiveness portion of the workshop: whether it was to use the restroom, make an important call, or just leave the room. Magically, those roaming students returned once the forgiveness section was complete and we moved onto a different topic.

The fact that some of my students were uncomfortable just hearing about forgiveness is when I realized the process of forgiveness can be too painful for a lot of people.

This is also when I realized the *power* of forgiveness, which is why I've been promoting the power of forgiveness for decades. I personally witnessed a significant transformation in numerous individuals who had endured lifelong pain, as they found the strength to forgive and move forward.

You may be wondering if my students were able to maintain the forgiveness of those who wronged them.

Or did my students move back into anger?

Some students were able to maintain the forgiveness, some didn't.

In 2023, I discovered the secret to ultimate forgiveness.

The crucial step that everyone overlooks that allows people to actually stay forgiven.

The step that ensures lasting, ultimate forgiveness.

CHAPTER 3

*"Forgiveness does not mean ignoring what has been done
or putting a false label on an evil act. It means, rather,
that the evil act no longer remains as a barrier to the
relationship. Forgiveness is a catalyst creating the
atmosphere necessary for a fresh start and a new
beginning."*

Martin Luther King Jr.

Before we talk about the Forgiveness Matrix™ lets chat about what anger does to you.

Pick up a glass and fill it with any kind of liquid: water, iced tea, or soda. Now hold the filled glass in front of you with your arm straight out and maintain your pose for a few minutes.

Your filled glass represents your emotions about your pain. The liquid inside your glass represents years and years of deeply held negative emotions like fear, resentment, and anger for all the things people have done or not done to you. For many, it has taken a long time to fill your glass of anger, and for others the glass was filled yesterday.

When you first begin feeling those negative emotions, it's *really* easy to hold the glass up, right? You can balance your life with your strong emotions because they are not affecting where you are going. The filled glass is manageable. However, the longer that you hold the glass, the more your arm will tire and eventually hurt.

Soon, your arm is going to start to ache, and holding on to that filled glass is becoming increasingly harder and harder.

When you first lifted it, you could easily hold it off to the side, but now that your arm is hurting, it's too painful. In fact, you can't focus on anything but the glass anymore. The weight of the glass grows heavier over time, affecting every part of your life, and the pain becomes more than you can bear. You talk about the heavy burden to everyone: crying, whining, yelling, screaming, and shouting to all who can hear you. You're also growing resentful about the fact that you have to hold the darn glass.

The glass of pain has wormed its way into every part of your life now. The longer you hold onto the glass, the heavier it gets, and the more painful it becomes.

After a while, you have to use your other arm to help hold the glass.

Now, look at your body language. Holding the glass of pain hasn't stopped your life *exactly* because you can still *sort of* see beyond it as you hold the glass in front of you. However, your life is negatively affected because both arms are now dedicated to holding the glass.

If you continue to hold the glass of pain, and you don't forgive those who harmed you, eventually your glass of pain is going to affect your life because it's always directly in front of you. The pain is now so intense it is all you see. You can't hold your glass off to the side any longer.

If you're stubborn and refuse to let go of the pain, thinking you can manage it all, after a while your little glass of pain is going to grow into a pitcher.

The pitcher is worse because what you are holding is so large it is now all you can see. You're missing opportunities being presented to you.

Your soul mate might have just walked into the room, but because you're holding on to your pitcher of emotions, you can't see your ideal mate and they walk away.

Your dream job, a potential new and fabulous house, a cure for your illness, or a great life-changing opportunity could all appear in front of you, and you won't see any of them because you're still focused on the pitcher.

Ideas, things, people, places, none of those opportunities are going to happen because all you can focus on is that which you're stubbornly holding. Your entire life is now focused on your painful emotions inside your pitcher: fear, anger, hatred, and resentments.

What's inside your pitcher of pain?

Does your pain stem from your childhood? From anyone in particular? From something someone did or didn't do? Are you resentful because you are sick, lonely, or hungry?

Whatever the reason, your pain is holding you back.

How do you get rid of the painful emotions inside the pitcher?

You already know the answer.

Forgiveness.

You might have to experience some mental gymnastics to get to a place where you can forgive them, but trust me, the outcome makes the process worth it.

Forgiveness allows you to toss out that burden of resentment and makes you feel lighter somehow.

Now, please allow me to be completely clear here.

As I said before, forgiving someone does **NOT** mean they were right, nor does it mean that you want a relationship with them. Forgiving someone means that there are less negative emotions in your glass, and you can finally put down the glass. You might not want to talk to the person who caused your pain, and that's fine! You don't have to call or go see those who caused you pain.

For me, forgiveness is intensely private and personal.

How do you know the forgiveness process worked?

You can look at their name without experiencing those painful emotions.

After you forgive, check your body language. With the glass down, you can finally see clearly all around you. Your hands are now free for you to do things. You see the opportunities flowing to you. Ideas will now flood your brain, and new roads will appear in your path.

Why?

The ideas were always there, they were just being stopped by your pain. You unconsciously pushed any new ideas away because your focus was the pain inside the glass. You lived it and breathed it every day.

So put down your glass of anger.

It's time, don't you think?

You have suffered enough.

Forgive the people who caused the pain inside the glass.

Release yourself and forgive. You forgive people for YOUR peace, not theirs.

Forgiveness breaks the tie that binds you to the pain maker and will allow you to stop focusing on the pain they caused.

Peace is good right?

Wouldn't a little peace be nice right now?

Who should you forgive first?

The person you are thinking about right now as you read these words.

Author's Note: For anyone who has read my book "Rainbows and Banana Peels," yes there is a chapter in there that talks about your glass of anger. It's such a great analogy I'm using it again here.

CHAPTER 4

"Forgiving isn't something you do for someone else. It's something you do for yourself. It's saying, 'You're not important enough to have a stranglehold on me.' It's saying, 'You don't get to trap me in the past. I am worthy of a future'."

Jodi Picoult

Thousands of books and articles have been written about forgiveness and its benefits. So why do people have such a hard time with it? Some can't forgive because the person or act was unforgivable.

That's fair.

Others simply don't want to forgive. They want to keep their pain. It's become a part of who they are. A part of their soul, if you will. Besides, if they forgive, then people will stop sympathizing with them. They won't get the attention anymore and then who would they be?

While forgiveness can be a healing and liberating act, the inability to forgive can cripple people and prevent them from moving forward in their life.

Why won't people forgive?

Below are a few reasons people have given me for not forgiving, and my responses.

If I am angry then I can't be hurt again. My anger protects me.

- *Suppressed anger is toxic and will lead to a host of physical issues including stress, which is also toxic.*

If I forgive them then that means the other person was right and they were not right!

- *No, it doesn't mean they were correct. It means you wish to be free.*

If I forgive them, then I have to tell them I forgive them, and I really don't want to do that.

- *No, you don't have to contact them. Forgiveness is personal.*

The person I need to forgive is dead, so it's too late.

- *It's not too late to forgive people who have already passed on.*

To forgive, then I will have to remember my horrible dysfunctional childhood. It's too painful for me.

- *I understand that you don't want to remember your dysfunctional childhood, but forgiving it will allow the pain of the memories to dissipate forever. You won't have to go back there ever again if you don't want to. For me personally, I now remember the good times. The bad? I find it really hard to dredge those memories up.*

It's important to remember that forgiveness is a gradual and very personal process and may take time, but ultimately, it leads to emotional liberation, inner peace, and joy.

CHAPTER 5

NAVIGATING THE TOUGH TERRAIN OF LETTING GO

"It's not an easy journey, to get to a place where you forgive people. But it is such a powerful place, because it frees you."

Tyler Perry

In 2020, I received news that a childhood father-figure conned my mother 30 years ago. It took many years, but the truth finally floated to the top. As if the 2020 pandemic wasn't challenging enough!

I had to wait until now to write about it.

Why? Quite simply, the memory of his betrayal was too difficult for me. I had to banish the whole thing from my thoughts for a while.

Then I had to forgive him.

Which was seriously hard.

I remember the day when we found out about his betrayal. It was the day we discovered that a painting he bought for my late mother was a fake. Then we learned the watch he gave her was also a fake.

Everything he gave her was fake.

The memory of my childhood father figure was suddenly ripped from me and a stranger was standing there instead.

It was all a lie!

Anger and pain flooded my body as the reality I remembered completely disappeared. The man was a father-figure for me during high school and the betrayal was crushing.

As friends and family supported me, I quietly fell apart, which was unusual as I rarely crumble. Even through stage 3 breast cancer I somehow managed to keep my footing. My motto was (and still is) "we can't always control what happens to us, but we sure can control how we get through it."

This time was different though. I felt like someone had thrown me to the ground so hard that it took all my breath out of my body. You may have experienced something as devastating in your life as well.

You really only have two choices when you feel like you've been thrown to the ground. You can stay down there, or you can get up.

Although I usually choose to get up, this time I decided to stay down there and let the emotions flow through me. Betrayal, anger, sadness … all of those painful emotions. I didn't stuff them down inside me like I normally did. Instead I faced them head on and allowed myself to fall.

That was a day of discovery for me as I let the feelings freely flow out of me. I didn't do it alone. I quietly reached out to my inner circle of friends and family to help me sort through the memories. It felt like a huge hair ball I needed to cough up and clear. As the day progressed, I choked on the feelings, and hated every minute of it. Deep down though I knew those painful feelings had to be released.

On the second day, the emotions began to clear. I spent most of the day working on mentally standing up again.

I reached for a few techniques that have worked well for me over the years.

- I looked at all the love in my life. Love from family and friends. Then I wrote it all down in a journal so I could look at the list again and again.

- I listened to music. When a song hit a nerve, I hit the repeat button. Sometimes more than once!
- I took a long walk to clear my head.
- I talked, vented, and cried with my good friend Katie. Then we tapped. *(Emotional Freedom Technique or EFT is a brain-based somatic technique which removes emotional blockages. You can reach her at her website at* <u>*www.Nalledgeco.com*</u>*).*

On the third day, I woke up feeling better. Lighter somehow. Even the house looked brighter to me.

I knew that I had to forgive him some day, but I wasn't ready yet. Instead, I did what I always do, I wrote an article about the experience. Although I never finished it, I saved it to my archive files, and then promptly forgot about it. My thought was that someday I might use the article in a book or something. It felt liberating to just write about it and release the emotions on paper.

Did I finally forgive him?

Yes, but it took me two years.

In 2022, I was looking in the "article" folder on my computer to see if I could find something for my monthly newsletter "The Thriving Times." As I glanced through the list, I noticed the article about my mother's friend.

I stared at the article for a very long time.

Eventually I decided that enough time had passed and forgave him using The Forgiveness Matrix™ defined in this book.

It would have been easy to let my anger and resentment become my new normal. I could have easily moved these emotions into my daily routine. The pain from his betrayal was all I could think about for days.

Instead, I went deep inside myself where it was calm, like the bottom of the ocean. It was in my internal secret place I could finally release the pain and find peace and love again.

As I look back on my childhood now, I focus on the love that was there. I remember the good things that happened. As for the rest? I am choosing to let it go.

Am I angry at him anymore?

No.

Am I still angry about my dysfunctional childhood?

No.

My feelings of anger and resentment are completely gone.

Today I can easily reflect and see the love that was in my past. I was too angry to see the love before because the pain was in my way.

That, my friend, is the kind of lasting peace I offer to you in this book.

CHAPTER 6

"Though I was unaware of it at the time, that simple act of forgiveness was the beginning of an entirely new level of experiencing life for me."

Wayne Dyer

"*You know, Katharine, I understand what you're saying, but I already did forgive them"* you might now be saying to me.

Yes. Yes you did.

Consider this though. If you really *have* completely forgiven them, then why are they entering your mind now as you read these words?

When you go on social media, and you see one of their posts, do ugly thoughts come up?

Or do you just snort and keep going.

If you see them fail at something, do you quietly smirk?

You see them in the grocery store, what do you do? Walk up to them or avoid them at all costs?

Do you still tell the story about what happened between you two?

You know the one. It doesn't matter if you spin it to be funny, the fact is you are still telling it, and the anger is still lurking behind it.

If you said yes to any of these statements, then you might want to forgive them one more time.

Listen, I told my "stories" for years. I hung onto them like an old pair of jeans that don't fit anymore. It felt so good when I finally threw them out!

To <u>completely</u> forgive those who caused you pain, to get them totally out of your mind, you will want to complete the entire Forgiveness Matrix™ detailed in this book.

It took me a long time to realize you just can't forgive some people right away. For the most painful hurts it's a process that takes time to release. Please be kind to yourself as you progress and grow. You'll move on when you are ready.

Katharine Giovanni

www.KatharineGiovanni.com

> ❝
>
> Here's the secret sauce:
>
> To truly forgive someone, and I mean really forgive so they stay forgiven, you also forgive the ENERGY around the person, place, or event.
>
> **KATHARINE GIOVANNI** ❞

CHAPTER 7

"Holding a grudge doesn't make you strong; it makes you bitter. Forgiving doesn't make you weak; it sets you free."

Dave Willis

What about that person, place, or event that was super horrible? The one that doesn't deserve to be forgiven. What about those memories?

It's **REALLY HARD** to forgive the unforgiveable.

Sometimes it isn't even appropriate. The evil of the situation is too much.

So what do you do?

You work with the *energy* around the unforgiveable.

Stay with me. I'll explain in a minute.

When someone or something is so awful and you absolutely positively cannot forgive it, then the only thing you CAN forgive is yourself and the energy around the actual event.

Someday in the future you might be able to return and forgive the person.

Maybe.

Some people can.

It's all good if you can't.

Forgiving yourself and the **energy** around the event will neutralize the painful energy and will help you move forward and heal.

Gratitude will help neutralize it as well.

How?

Well, sometimes the only lesson you can see is what the experience taught you **not** to do, or who **not** to be. Perhaps it showed you how much strength and courage you have. Or it showed you who your real friends were.

At the end of the day, that's still gratitude, right?

Gratitude is your armor against hate and negativity.

The experience provided you with contrast so you would recognize good.

Also, please forgive yourself for all the unhealthy habits and traits you picked up when you were enduring that trauma. Forgive yourself for becoming the person you needed to be in order to endure and survive.

As you consider the most painful memories on your forgiveness list, forgive yourself for any role you may have played good or bad, and then forgive the energy around the entire situation.

In the future you might be able to return and process the Forgiveness Matrix™ on this person again.

Then again you may not.

It's all good.

As I said before, some things are unforgiveable.

Forgive what you can and move on with your life.

CHAPTER 8

*"I think the first step is to understand that forgiveness does
not exonerate the perpetrator. Forgiveness liberates the
victim. It's a gift you give yourself."*

T.D. Jakes

In addition to forgiving people, you can forgive
locations, events, and even energy!

Uh, what?

You can forgive locations?

You can forgive events?

Absolutely.

In addition to people, you can absolutely forgive
events, places, and even specific months or years.

Personally, I forgave the year 1974. That entire year was horrible. Good riddance to it I say. I forgave it because I was tired of it hanging around in my mind.

I have also forgiven schools I attended, buildings where I worked, and even cities where I lived. Forgiving these locations brought me peace.

You might now be asking…

What do you mean when you say you can forgive energy?

Stay with me on this.

According to Albert Einstein, "Energy cannot be created or destroyed, it can only be changed from one form to another."

Science has also shown us that people, plants, and animals all emit energy. Essentially, the energy around our body is an electromagnetic field that has its own unique vibration.

Vibrations that people can feel.

Since energy cannot be destroyed, energy that is caused by negative emotions will stay in our energy field until we clear it.

Forgiveness releases that painful energy from our bodies.

Ancient Chinese culture understood this vital energy really well as they both developed and integrated various practices such as Qigong and Acupuncture into their healthcare.

Similarly, various nations across the globe have developed healing traditions that harness the body's energies, including practices such as yoga, martial arts, and meditation, among others. These traditions are evident in nations such as India, Tibet, Egypt, Thailand, Japan, and among many Native American cultures, to name a few.

There is also Reiki. A practice that originated in Japan in the early twentieth century. Reiki practitioners believe there is a universal life energy that flows through all living beings. An energy they can harness and use for healing.

Scientific principles show that our universe consists of energy vibrating at various frequencies. Thoughts and emotions also produce their own energy vibrations. Therefore, when we concentrate our thoughts on specific subjects, they send out unique signals that draw in similar-frequency energies with similar vibrations.

Simply stated, like-energy attracts like-energy.

Staying with me so far?

If you are angry and resentful, you will attract more situations, people, or circumstances that align with that vibrational energy.

Not exactly what you're looking to attract right?

Dr. Masaru Emoto, a Japanese researcher, conducted groundbreaking experiments that demonstrated how emotions affect water molecules. His research revealed the ability of words to change the molecular composition of water.

Dr. Emoto proved that when water was exposed to expressions of love, gratitude, and positivity, it responded in kind by creating clear and beautiful crystals. When the water was exposed to expressions of hatred or negativity, however, it formed distorted and ugly formations.

These experiments provide tangible proof that water has an awareness that can be altered by our words and sounds.

Therefore, since the human body is, on average, over 60% water, imagine what forgiveness can do to it. Imagine what it will do to the cells within your body!

At the very least, I'll bet you'll feel better.

Here's another example of the effects of energy.

An experiment at a school in the United Arab Emirates called "Bully A Plant" highlighted the harmful results of negative comments.

IKEA, a furniture retailer, placed two identical plants at a school and asked students to compliment one while bullying the other for 30 days. The experiment was for Anti-Bullying Day. Though IKEA acknowledged it wasn't an "objective" scientific experiment, both plants were kept in controlled environments with equal water, nutrition, and sun. Students' comments were transmitted directly to the plants via speakers.

It shouldn't surprise you that after one month, the plant that received compliments displayed a healthy and happy appearance while the one receiving negativity was wilting and sick.

Personally, I've been talking to plants for years. One of my plants, that we lovingly call Grandpa, has been with us for over 27 years! Sure do hope he has a few more good years in him.

So what does this exercise tell us?

If water and plants can be negatively impacted by negative energy, and positive words cause them to thrive then imagine how it impacts humans!

In her book "Unconditional Forgiveness," Mary Hayes Greco tells us that the act of forgiving and releasing negative energy can significantly improve your health. By letting go of stagnant energy and allowing fresh energy to flow to you, forgiveness plays a role in fostering a feeling of physical rejuvenation.

Forgiveness not only has physical benefits for your body, but it can help you move past a situation more permanently and relieve yourself of its weight.

If forgiving a **person** makes such a difference to your body and life, can you imagine what forgiving the **energy** around your body might do?

CHAPTER 9

"If you want to find the secrets of the universe, think in terms of energy, frequency, and vibration."

Nikola Tesla

Is forgiveness always easy or quick?

No, not always.

Be kind to yourself as forgiveness is a process. It's a marathon, not a sprint. And the result is your personal peace which is totally worth the effort!

Right now you are probably making a mental list of the people you've forgiven more than once, and yet you still don't have that peace I'm talking about.

You might be wondering what you're doing wrong.

Why does their name zing your brain every darn time you see it?

You didn't forgive the energy.

The pain is still hanging around in your energy field and it's tripping you up. In short, the painful emotion is affecting your body's vibration.

A vibration people can feel.

So what happens to anger when the pain energy leaves your body? Many of us assume that it just goes out into the universe and dissipates right?

Sadly no.

Painful emotions are stubborn and will stay in your energy field until you clear it. Eventually your energy field will get dark and toxic wreaking havoc on your life like a bull in a China shop.

Your body consists of energy-producing particles that are in constant motion. So YOU are vibrating and creating energy every second.

I remember when I first stumbled across vibrational energy.

I was 24 years old and working as an assistant to a meeting planner for a non-profit association in New York City.

One bright and sunny morning, a new employee arrived at the office. She was smiling and politely shaking everyone's hand.

Not surprisingly, her name was Karen.

When she approached me, she smiled, greeted me politely, and shook my hand. I smiled back and welcomed her to the team. I then watched as the color completely drained from her face. She immediately withdrew her hand from mine and proceeded to take a giant step backwards as if she had just seen a ghost.

I tried to shrug her strange behavior off when I returned to my desk, but it was just so darn odd!

For the next few months Karen often tried to get me in trouble. It appeared she hated my guts, which was odd as we rarely spoke to each other. Everyone in the office noticed, and not one of us could explain her behavior. Thank goodness the Internet was not around then as I can only imagine what she would have posted about me! Thankfully, she left the company the following year. I never could understand what I did to her.

Years later, I finally figured it out when I researched a concept called vibrational energy. It's the energy each of us projects and some of us can feel.

My *vibrational energy* made Karen feel uncomfortable.

It's extremely hard to be near someone who has a different level of vibrational energy than you. It's like oil and water and it's difficult to be near each other.

Now that I understand vibrational energy, I try to not take it personally when someone I meet doesn't want to be near me.

It's also the reason why some friendships end and marriages dissolve. The individual's energy shifts.

Once I figured out what was happening, I became curious and started paying attention to people's individual energy. Like the colors in a rainbow, I discovered that people project shades of vibrational energy.

Your vibrational energy affects everyone you meet, and every relationship you have. You can tolerate certain people because their vibrational energy is within a comfortable range. Others you can't tolerate because their vibrational level is so different from yours you literally can't stand next to them.

I have concluded the energy difference is the reason why some bullies pick on others. One person is uncomfortable with another person's energy level. So instead of walking away, they bully the other person. The bully can feel the energetic difference even if they can't understand it. They *feel* it in their core, and it feels bad to them. To make themselves feel better, and to control the situation, they bully others.

Over the years, I noticed that occasionally someone would shake my hand, give me a strange look, and then take a step away from me just like Karen did years before. It didn't bother me because deep down I knew it wasn't me personally, it was my energy, and it felt weird to them.

For instance, around 2010, a group of intuitive friends and I visited a restaurant. After the hostess sat us at a table, I noticed the server was avoiding us. Although it seemed odd at the time, I ignored her behavior as I thought she might just be busy. Eventually, the server came to our table to take our orders.

When she came to me, however, the color completely drained from her face. She then took two giant steps away from me.

I noticed her odd behavior and again brushed it off. Maybe she was having a bad day I thought. So remembering my concierge training, I smiled as broadly as I could and politely gave her my order.

A bit later she brought our food to our table. I watched as she politely gave everyone their lunch plates.

When she came to me, however, she threw my plate across the table like a frisbee. I'm not kidding! In fact, she threw it so hard that the food bounced around on the plate. Her face white as a sheet, she looked at me like I was the devil incarnate and ran back to the kitchen.

I fully expected her to come back and sprinkle me with holy water.

After she left, one of my friends leaned over and whispered, "she's afraid of your energy."

Ah yes! I had forgotten about the "Karen" incident years before and immediately understood. I was really tempted to say "boo" to her when she returned with the check. However, my concierge training kicked in again, so I merely smiled at her.

Did she smile back? Absolutely not. Just stared at me like I was a character from a Steven King novel.

Over the years, I occasionally noticed someone acting strangely around me. They would either ignore me to the point where they treated me as if I were invisible, or they would physically run the other way.

I would just shake it off and keep going.

Another more recent example includes my husband, Ron. We had been thinking about moving to the mountains.

We spent a lovely weekend in Ashville, NC to learn more about the city. On our second day, we visited a neighborhood we had researched online.

As Ron drove through the gates, the energy of the place hit me immediately, and it felt really uncomfortable. I ignored the feeling as I wanted to like this place. Yet as we drove around, I just couldn't shake the feeling that something was seriously off.

The neighborhood was built on the side of a mountain. So all the homes had steep stairs. The locale was definitely not a good place for my husband who has had over a dozen knee operations.

Knowing we were not going to live there, Ron decided to stop by the sales office anyways as he had spoken to the woman before and wanted to say hello.

The sales office was on the second floor of a small building with a wraparound porch. Ron and I stood there a moment trying to decide if I should run upstairs (since my knees are fine) to see if the realtors would come down and say hello.

Just as I was about to walk upstairs, a woman popped her head out from her upstairs office. She didn't come down, just said "Hello."

Ron replied back and politely asked if he could have a sales packet. He's a realtor and thought it might come in handy.

The realtor stared at us for a good minute or two. It was as if she was trying to decide if she wanted to come downstairs or not. She then ducked back inside her office. The next thing I know she is coming down the stairs with a small teacup dog strapped to her chest in a sling. We politely introduced ourselves and started asking a few questions.

The whole thing felt off to me.

REALLY off.

The energy just didn't feel right. I also noticed she was standing far away from me. I ignored it thinking it must have something to do with the little dog.

Then the sales manager appeared on the balcony, took one look at us, waived, and said she had a client coming and was sorry she couldn't come down.

That was the last straw for me. Between the uncomfortable energy feeling and the awful customer service, my brain just about exploded.

I've been training concierge and front-line staff all over the world for over 25 years. I know that good customer service means coming down those freaking stairs, shake the potential client's hands, and then when your clients arrive (which they did a few minutes later), personally escort them upstairs to your office. This way you politely greet two potential clients at the same time.

We quickly ended the conversation by thanking them for the information and drove away.

We couldn't get away fast enough.

Not surprisingly, the minute we drove back through the gates, the uncomfortable energy feeling disappeared.

The next morning it hit me like a bolt of lightning.

It was my vibrational energy again!

My energy, combined with Ron's, must have made the realtors uncomfortable. The first realtor protected herself by strapping a little dog to her chest. The sales manager's solution was to refuse to come down the stairs at all.

In fact, the energy of the neighborhood was so different from ours that we both felt a little ill while we were there.

On the other side of the coin, I often find myself surrounded by strangers when I shop. Why? Some people are attracted to my energy level. I can be shopping in an empty aisle and then get halfway down, and all types of people decide to shop in the same aisle.

It happens to me in other stores as well. The store can be empty when we arrive, and filled with people when we leave.

I often wonder if I should send them an invoice for getting people to come into their store!

I can't tell you how many people walk into my house and ask me why it feels so good.

It's the energy.

Author's Note: You might have noticed the anger lurking behind that last story about the saleswoman with her little dog. Even after all this time, anger still rears its head.

My editor noticed the energy of the paragraph when she was editing. We kept the story exactly as I originally wrote it to demonstrate to you that someone, or something, will always have the ability to make you angry. It's part of being human. What you DO with that anger, is the question.

For me personally, once the painful tone of the story was pointed out, I immediately did the Forgiveness Matrix™ in the back of this book. Truth be told, I do the forgiveness mantra often as situations arise.

So how often should you do the Forgiveness Matrix™?

As many times as you need to. Hourly, daily, weekly, monthly… it depends on which memory is affecting you.

CHAPTER 10

"Hating someone makes them important. Forgiving them makes them obsolete."

Author Unknown

The reality of life is that some people, locations, and events are harder to forgive than others. Like many of us, you might have a few people you will never forgive, and that's fine because you'll discover peace from forgiving other aspects of the pain they caused.

I've forgiven individuals, groups of people, places, events, and even years. As I said earlier, I actually sat down and forgave the entire year of 1974 – everything that happened that year and all the people who were in my life at the time.

Since it's a long story, here's the short version. I was in the eighth grade, getting bullied almost every day, my parents were going through an ugly divorce, and I attempted suicide.

The entire year was hell.

Is it crazy that I had to forgive something that happened to me decades ago?

Not at all. I held on to that 1974 anger for decades. It was my story. It became who I was.

I was a survivor!

I proudly wore that title for years. Until I was ready to move on from it.

Eventually I learned that it was holding me back, so I decided to get rid of it.

You see forgiveness is personal. Really personal. You do it only for you. You forgive so you can be released from the pain you are living with.

Forgiveness is **NOT** for those who caused the pain.

It's never for them.

It's all for you.

In fact, many of them probably don't even know what they did, nor do they care. Even if they do know, they're most likely not thinking about you at all.

But admit it, YOU think about it.

In fact, you think about it all the time. You're obsessed with it. It's an ever-growing ball of pain you just can't get rid of.

Quite simply you may feel as if you are in hell, holding your giant ball of negative emotions.

You ARE in hell.

I've been there once or twice myself actually.

You might be thinking ... for the second time in this book.

But Katharine, I really did forgive them. Why do it again?

Absolutely you forgave them.

Here is where the Forgiveness Matrix™ will complete the final steps of forgiveness while taking all aspects of the pain you're feeling into consideration.

You see, saying the words "I forgive you" may complete what everyone believes is required, and yet you may not feel the internal peace that everyone talks about.

Why?

Mostly because there are still emotions associated with the painful memory.

As you move forward, you may feel that the weight of the anger and resentment is not noticeable, when in reality your body has just become numb to the pain. You almost don't feel it anymore but trust me because it's still there. It's only after you forgive ALL aspects of the pain that you will feel total and complete peace with no emotion associated to the situation.

Why?

Feelings are a form of energy.

An energy that sticks around in your energy field like glue.

Keeping positive emotions in your energy field is fantastic, but the negative ones? Those little suckers will bring you to your knees and break you if you let them.

Forgiveness transforms the negative energy feelings into positive ones.

This is exactly why I want you to forgive the *energy* around the memory whether it was a person, a location, or an event.

Clearing the energy around the memory allows you to finally release that ball of pain you've been carrying around.

Remember that pitcher of anger and pain I spoke about in an earlier chapter? You'll be able to release your pitcher of resentment, pain, and anger.

I suggest you start with the least painful ones, the easy-to-forgive people.

You know the ones I'm talking about.

It's the grade school kid who stole your lunch, or how about the time when you were ten and your friend borrowed your favorite shirt and ruined it?

You loved that shirt!

I recommend starting with the easy ones to forgive.

For me, the forgiveness process was quick for a few people on my list, and others took weeks/months/years. I got there eventually, and you will, too.

Save the most painful events and people for later as they might take more time to forgive all aspects. You might have to forgive those in layers. Similar to peeling layers from an onion, with time, you will eventually get to peace.

Be kind to yourself during this process. You'll get there, and trust me, the process is totally worth it!

When I did these forgiveness exercises, it felt like I was walking out of a black fog as I released the grip on my pitcher of anger. I could see where I was going again! I could love again. I could even like myself. The world got brighter, my overall health improved, and my finances got better.

At the time, I didn't understand why forgiving someone affected all these other areas in my life, yet it did.

It took time to work through the list of people I needed to forgive to feel my internal peace. For the more painful ones, like my parents, it took a few years. Sometimes you have to forgive people more than once, especially if they are family.

You may be wondering, *"What if I see some of the people on my list every day?"*

You might have to forgive them more than once depending on the situation, and that's fine.

The good news is that you'll be more positive and will feel better, which might irritate your hater a bit. A little side entertainment for you <grin>.

Or you may be wondering, *"What if the person has died, do I still have to forgive them?"*

You absolutely can forgive them even if they have already passed. Remember you forgive for **you**, not them. If their name appears on your list of people to forgive, then absolutely you should forgive them.

In the end, since this is all about you, where they are, or aren't, is meaningless really.

Ratings

Throughout this book, I've been suggesting to you that you forgive the least painful memory, or the "easy" ones first, and then work your way up to the most painful memories.

How do you decide which memories are the least (or most) painful?

Well, how badly are those events interfering with your life? Only a little or a lot?

In the Forgiveness Matrix™, you will rate memories on a scale between one (1) and ten (10), with a ten (10) being the most painful.

Easy – Ratings between one (1) and three (3)

Easy memories involve people who don't really interfere with your everyday life.

They are the people who took your parking space at the grocery store. Or it's something, or someone, from your childhood that still irritates you when the memory pops up.

How about the girl who ruined your sweater in college? Or the lawn guy who didn't show up the other day?

People who made you feel angry in the moment.

People who you are easily forgiven.

On the worksheet in the back of this book, I would rate these memories between one (1) and three (3), with one (1) being the least painful.

You might not even be mad anymore, but their name has already formed in your mind as you read these words. Write the name on your Forgiveness Worksheet anyways.

Medium – Ratings between four (4) and seven (7)

The medium memories interfere with your life in some way.

Those are the memories of people and events that creep into your mind more and more as the days go by. Especially when you see something, or someone, who reminds you of them.

You can stuff the memory back into the corners of your mind for a while, but they're persistent little buggers as they always manage to come into your memory again.

You occasionally tell people the story behind it and often allow your pain to come through when you do.

You see the perpetrator's name in an email, call, text message, or social media post and it zings your brain to recall the event.

You've forgiven many of those who hurt you, but the forgiveness didn't seem to stick. You still have painful emotions about them. You're bitter, angry, and irritated with them on some level.

The painful memories which earned a rating of four or five are close to permanent forgiveness. If you forgive the energy around these people, you'll get closer to your internal peace. It might not happen in the first round of forgiveness, but you'll get there if you keep at it.

As I've said before, forgiveness is like an onion with many layers. The more parts of the memory you forgive, the closer to the center of peace you'll get.

Hard – Ratings between eight (8) and ten (10)

These are the memories you are absolutely <u>NOT</u> ready to forgive.

They hurt you deeply and the pain is still raw.

The unforgivable are in this group. They're the ones you rate a ten (10).

Eventually, you might be able to forgive the memories in this group. Then again, you might not. It's all good either way.

Forgiving yourself and the energy around the memory is the key to unlocking the pain from this group.

When you forgive yourself and the energy around it, you'll remove the first layer of pain. Later, you return and keep taking cracks at the pain. By doing this, you're slowly trimming off the layers of pain which will eventually get you to the center.

Please be aware that the process to forgive your "hard" ones might take weeks or months to reduce to a medium level memory. You might even move them to "easy" and be able to forgive the memories at some point.

That's what happened with my parents. Took me a while to forgive them down to an "easy" level where I could finally forgive them.

A few of your memories may never be forgiven.

They're unforgiveable.

And that's fine.

As I've said before, simply forgive the energy around the memory and move on with your life.

It's all good. I promise.

What happens when you forgive a memory?

Does the energy move?

The short answer is yes. Energy moves both inside and outside of you.

Do you remember the childhood friend I wrote about earlier in this book? They're the one that had the figurine I gave them 'mysteriously' fall to the ground just when I was forgiving them.

When I did this exercise, I rated the pain they inflicted on me as a one (1). So if a "one" can move a figurine to the ground, can you imagine what the energy from those higher scored memories will do?

Yes, not only will you notice a difference in your energy, but forgiveness affects others as well.

CHAPTER 11

"Forgiveness is a strange thing. It can sometimes be easier to forgive our enemies than our friends. It can be hardest of all to forgive people we love."

Fred Rogers

With all this background information, you are ready for the details of how to forgive. It's more than just repeating the words, "I forgive."

The Forgiveness Matrix™ includes forgiving situations, locations, people, yourself, and the energy around each one of these. All these items need to be forgiven for the peace you deserve.

How do you start the Forgiveness Matrix™?

Slowly my friend. Slowly.

Remember the parable about the tortoise and the hare? The tortoise won! Slow and steady wins the race. And slow and steady is critical as you begin forgiving the memories on your list.

This is a marathon not a sprint.

I suggest you first identify the person, place, and situation you wish to forgive. Be as detailed as possible when you begin.

Let's start with an easy example.

For instance, let's recall being in middle school when someone you thought was a friend, didn't invite you to their party. Specifically, the person to forgive would be the friend who didn't invite you. Let's call that person Terry.

First, identify how it made you feel. Which emotion comes up? Can you move past your feelings after all these years?

Absolutely you can.

Then, using the mantra in this chapter, you should forgive your "friend" Terry, the party, the location, yourself, and the energy around each of these items.

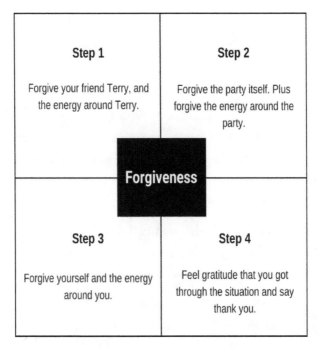

When I did this exercise, I wrote down every painful memory that I could think of. Every event, every situation, every person, every place I could recall.

I randomly wrote whatever name appeared in my mind. I wrote the name down even if it was an object or a building.

Then, I rated them individually giving each of them a number between one (1) and ten (10).

Once the memories were rated, I recited the Forgiveness Mantra for each one.

I quickly learned to never forgive more than ten (10) memories in 24 hours. *(I'll tell you why in a moment.)* I usually did them at night right before I went to sleep so my body had time to recover.

You may be excited to get this Forgiveness Matrix™ started and want to forgive more than ten (10) memories at once. Trust me, especially at the beginning, please limit your forgiveness to no more than ten (10) because of the energy exchange that will occur.

Whenever I do this mantra, I feel the energy change in the center of my chest as I forgive someone. I feel movement there. Pressure. Like something just left my body.

It's a feeling.

This is my personal sign I've forgiven them. You may feel energy change in your body as well, or not. It's a very personal experience. Just pay attention to your body after you forgive people.

The feeling of pressure leaving my body is how I personally know I have forgiven someone. I am very sensitive to energy.

What happens when I don't feel that energy?

For me, I know that I have a bit more work to do, so I'll forgive the energy and then try again in a day or two.

When you forgive a memory you may (or may not) feel the energy like I do. If you don't, no worries! Not everyone does. Some people just feel better. Others feel a tiny bit happier. You might feel a pressure somewhere in your body. Simply pay attention after you do a few so you recognize your personal signal.

You also might also feel tired after the Forgiveness Matrix™ exercise, or you might have other physical reactions like a headache or stomachache. Some people are in the bathroom for a bit, to put it delicately. Not to worry, that's just your body's way of clearing all the negative emotions out of your body. Allow it to happen. It won't last forever, and you'll feel better after the process is complete.

This is also why I want to limit you to forgiving a maximum of ten (10) people a day. Your body needs time to recover! If you do more than ten, then there's a good chance you'll make yourself sick.

This is powerful stuff.

Trust me. I tried doing more than ten once. I sat there and must have forgiven dozens of people and places in one sitting.

What happened?

I spent the next 48 hours in bed, dizzy and exhausted, with some really bad stomach issues. Everyone thought I had caught a stomach bug of some sort.

It wasn't a bug.

I just forgave too many people at once and my body had to take some time to release all the negative energy.

Please show yourself compassion. You're still here and you're fine. Remember, as of this minute, whoever or whatever you're forgiving is in the past now, and the past can't hurt you.

Whatever pain I felt after saying the mantra, I wrote it on my worksheet. You can write your list all at once, or over the course of several days.

Your worksheets are in the appendix at the end of this book to help you. For example, I wrote down:

- **Events,** events such as the 8th grade when I almost committed suicide. Anything that created pain and made you angry, resentful, or unhappy.
- **Relationships** that went sour.
- **Individual** people including friends, family, co-workers, clients.
- **Groups** of people such as the girls who bullied me in elementary school.

- **Places** that brought me negative thoughts including companies, buildings, cities, and even a particular year (like 1974 for example).
- **Myself!** This one was hard depending on what event/person I was thinking about.
- **Feelings**. I wrote down how I felt about each one. Although I tried to write one or two emotions, for a few people it turned into a paragraph, which I never sent. Felt good to get it out though! Remember, this process is super personal and doesn't require you to share anything with anyone.

ANYTHING that came into my mind, I listed.

It doesn't matter one bit if other people have positive memories for a person or place, and you have negative ones.

Ignore that.

Let me say it again. You're changing the energy for YOU not them.

My friend Katie forgave a little red wagon from her childhood. When she was writing her list, she randomly wrote it down. Had no idea why and no memory of it! She did the mantra on it anyways because there was obviously an unconscious part of her that was still mad at the thing.

There is no right way or wrong way to do this, just list whatever causes you pain to recall.

Once you have identified who or what you want to forgive, you can begin the forgiveness process in the next chapter.

Gratitude

You will notice that I want you to say thank you and feel gratitude at the end of the mantra. Feeling gratitude towards the person, place, event, and yourself will propel you forward.

Surprised? I was too.

Gratitude is the healing balm to cure the pain. Trust me on this.

Can't feel gratitude? Too painful?

That's fair.

Just feel gratitude towards yourself for getting through it. That should be enough to push your energy forward a bit. Eventually you can return and try again.

I had to circle back for a few people on my list. Actually, to be completely fair, I had to return more than once.

What eventually got me to forgiveness was a passage from the Bible. To paraphrase, it basically says "please forgive them Father, they don't know what they're doing."

That phrase has stayed with me for years and is always how I forgive anyone with a rating of seven (7) or higher.

For example, how can I be mad at someone in elementary school for not knowing Geometry? They haven't learned it yet! How can I be angry at that? When I consider the pain of my childhood, I finally realized my parents did the best they could with the limited tools they had at their disposal. At the end of the day, I can forgive them. Was it good enough? No. But I'm at peace. They did the best they could. I am grateful to them for teaching me what NOT to do.

As I got to the bottom half of my list, I had a TON of people I had to return to forgive. How long did it take me to get through the entire list? A few months, years for two of them. Of course, I didn't know what tapping (EFT-Emotional Freedom Technique) was as I hadn't met my friend Katie yet, so I had to feel my way through by myself. Tapping would have sped up the process! Her contact information is in the appendix.

Again, please be kind to yourself. Show yourself some compassion. It's important and good practice to start with the least painful memories as forgiving them will help you begin to feel better!

Remember, you absolutely do **NOT** have to reach out to these people, although you can if you wish. This is something you are doing for you, NOT them.

Forgiveness is an intensely personal journey.

Forgiveness lightens your soul and returns you to peace.

Author's Note:

When I wrote the line *"events such as the 8th grade when I almost committed suicide,"* earlier in this chapter, I leaned back in my chair and stared at the words for a few minutes.

Almost immediately, I felt a wave of emotion coming from the past. I could actually feel how my family would have felt if I had died in the eighth grade. I felt their deep sadness, and waves of their emotions penetrated my heart like a knife. Tears flowed down my cheeks unchecked as I sat at my desk staring at the words on that page.

What a great gift! It's a moment I will never forget, and yes I did some forgiveness work on it as I sat there.

If you or someone you know could use mental health resources, please call 988, the National Suicide Prevention Lifeline at 800-273-8255, or the appropriate number in the country you live in.

You are worthy. You are loved. You matter. You mean something.

We want you to stay.

CHAPTER 12

"You can't forgive without loving. And I don't mean sentimentality. I don't mean mush. I mean having enough courage to stand up and say, 'I forgive. I'm finished with it'."

Maya Angelou

Everything on our planet has energy around it, and that energy can be forgiven and changed to a more positive form. As I've said many times in this book, forgiveness is very personal. You do it for YOU.

You can forgive anything: people, places, things, events, anything.

To begin, use the **Forgiveness Worksheets** I designed at the back of this book, or you can grab some paper and a pen and sit quietly for a few minutes. It all works.

Read the complete instructions below before you start the process.

To begin the Forgiveness Matrix, find a comfortable place where you can sit quietly uninterrupted. Leave behind all technology. Separate from all interruptions for a few minutes. Alert partners, children, friends, and pets you need uninterrupted time.

Lie on a bed, sit on your sofa, or find a nice tree outside – someplace you are comfortable..

Close your eyes.

Take three deep breaths.

Now ground yourself by imagining a white cord is going from the top of your head all the way up to the heavens.

Next, imagine your feet have tree roots attached to them descending down to the center of the earth.

Stay with me, even if you think those last two paragraphs were nuts.

Open your eyes and look at your Forgiveness List.

Select one of your least painful memories – one with a rating of a one (1).

Now visualize the person in your mind. Remember the circumstances. See it play out in your head like a movie. Don't assign any emotion into your reenactment.

Remember this is in your past where you have no power anymore.

Just breathe.

You're safe now.

In this place.

Right here.

You are safe.

The past cannot hurt you.

If you have trouble visualizing the person try this alternative process.

Place an empty chair in front of you and imagine the person is sitting there. Then talk to the chair. You can even put the person's picture on the chair if you like.

As you repeat the Forgiveness Mantra in this chapter, what emotions come up for that person? Write the associated emotion on your paper next to their name.

If it's a positive emotion, fantastic! You're done! Put a check mark next to their name.

If it's a negative one, then simply move on and try again later.

If you're using the "chair" method, when you have completely forgiven your perpetrator, then throw out the photo. What if you don't have a photo? Find something in your home that symbolizes the person, or Google a picture and print it out to use as a symbol.

FEEL the forgiveness in your heart.

Feel as if you've forgiven them.

Speak the words from your heart.

Now place your hand on your heart and recite the Mantra. Your hand is merely a reminder to speak from your heart.

Forgiveness is more about the feelings than the words. The words are just there to help you… the forgiveness emotion is the key.

The Process

Using the Mantra on the next page, here are the steps.

Step 1: You forgive the person and the energy around the person or event.

Pause. Feel the emotions that come up. Write them down on your worksheet/pad of paper.

Step 2: You forgive the event and the energy around the event.

Pause. Feel the emotions that come up. Write them down.

Step 3: You forgive yourself and the energy around you.

Pause before you open your eyes. How do you feel? Still angry? If that is the case, return to the process in a few days.

Step 4: Say "thank you." Sit for a second and feel gratitude that you are finally in a place where you can forgive them. You're finally free.

If this was a hard one, then feel gratitude that you're in a position to start the forgiveness process on this person/place/event. Congratulate yourself! This was a huge step!

The Mantra

> **I completely forgive <name/location/event.>**
> *Pause and breathe.*
> **I completely forgive the energy around <name/location/event.>**
> *Pause and breathe.*
> **I completely forgive myself and the energy around me.**
> *Pause and breathe.*
> **I completely forgive the energy around the entire situation(s) between us.**
> *Pause and breathe.*
> **Thank you.**
> *Sit for a second and feel gratitude that you are finally in a place where you can forgive them.*
> **And so it is.**

Forgiving the hard ones on the list

Did you lean into the emotion and find you are still angry and upset?

You don't think the mantra worked?

Was that name one of the more painful memories?

The Forgiveness Mantra worked. It's just this particular memory caused you so much pain that you'll have to chip away at it. Like I've said before, forgiveness can often be compared to an onion. You forgive the first layer, but there is more underneath. It might take a few rounds to get to the center.

So what should you do after repeating this process?

First, stand up, take a deep breath, and then walk around the room shaking your entire body like a dog shakes off water.

I'm serious about this one.

Animals shake to relieve anxiety. They literally shake off the old energy and tension as a way of resettling.

According to Roopali Shrivastava, counseling psychologist at IWill, "Animals don't get post-traumatic stress disorder (PTSD). The reason is, once out of danger, they shiver and shake and release the trauma from their bodies. Human beings develop PTSD because of frozen emotions."

If you continuously suppress your painful emotions, they will trap the negative energy inside of you. This will cause a bunch of not-so-nice things to happen to you such as illness, anxiety, and addiction to name a few.

So shake your body to relieve the anxiety and tension, and then do another round of forgiveness.

Only this time …

Forgive the energy only.

Don't say the person's name. Just forgive the energy around the situation. Then move on to the next name on your list. Return later.

How do I know when I've completely forgiven someone?

When I see their name on social media, or in a text/email/phone call and it doesn't zing my emotions like it normally does.

When I can look back at that memory and feel neutral emotions.

THAT'S when I know I'm finally free.

CHAPTER 13

"To forgive is to set a prisoner free and discover that the prisoner was you."

Lewis B. Smedes

You might be asking if you are done.

You've cleared painful memories. You've forgiven people, places, and energy, and have forgiven everyone and everything you could think of.

Are we done now?

No.

No, you're not.

If it makes you feel any better, I can always find people to forgive. Not so much from the distant past because I've moved on. Mine are more current.

Sadly, like me, you will never be completely done with forgiveness. We are humans after all, and humans irritate other humans. There will always be someone you need to forgive, including yourself.

Forgiveness is a marathon, not a sprint.

I used to be angry. REALLY angry.

At my birth family. At my life. At everyone.

My self-talk back then? It was horrific.

I hated my life.

I hated myself even more.

I happily wallowed in that for years.

Today?

I am at peace and I'm not angry anymore.

The anger is completely gone.

I can look at photographs from my past and not feel anger. I can see the names of those who hurt me and feel nothing at all.

I'm a totally different person.

Now please don't get me wrong here. Just because I forgave these people doesn't necessarily mean that I want a relationship with them. I don't, and that's fine.

Do things still make me angry? Are there people I probably should forgive?

Yes to both questions.

Will some of the people you've forgiven make you angry again?

Sure. Especially if they are family members.

This is exactly why I do these exercises a few times a year to make sure my anger energy stays neutralized. Sometimes, when someone trips me up, I have to say the forgiveness mantra daily for a while.

It happens.

The good news is that you're going to feel so much better after doing these exercises that you're never going to want to go back to the old you.

The new you feels too good!

What happens now?

LIFE happens.

LOVE happens.

Live your life to its fullest.

Bring joy and peace to others.

Be a light that people can follow.

Be a lighthouse and shine your light to guide others.

You totally got this my friend.

I believe in you.

Chapter 14

"As I walked out the door toward the gate that would lead to my freedom, I knew if I didn't leave my bitterness and hatred behind, I'd still be in prison."

Nelson Mandala

The Gratitude Exercise

First thing in the morning, or the last thing before you go to bed, write down the three greatest things that you are grateful for right now.

It doesn't have to be Moses parting the water stuff, it could be that you ate a great slice of pizza. If you want to list more than three, go for it.

Gratitude means appreciating the good things in life, no matter how big or small. Making the practice of gratitude a regular part of your day can build happiness, self-esteem, and provide other health benefits.

Just grab a pad of paper and a pen, or your phone/laptop if you prefer, and write the date and the words "today I am grateful for…." Try and write at least three every night. After 3 days, reread them! It will give you proof that there are positive things happening in your life, no matter how small.

If you really can't think of anything, answer a few of these questions instead.

One good thing that happened to me today was:

- My favorite part of today was:
- I had so much fun yesterday doing:
- I was so thankful yesterday for _____.

The Forgiveness Workbook

Instructions

The first worksheet is where you write all the painful memories you can recall. Don't judge, just write. It could be people's names, places you've been, buildings, objects, dates… it doesn't matter. Write down each of them no matter how weird they may seem to you.

Once the list is started, assign a rating next to each item from 1 to 10 with 10 being the most painful of the bunch. Write down as many painful memories as you like.

I always start with the least painful memories first and work my way up to the most painful ones.

Using the worksheets, start your Forgiveness Matrix™ with the people/places/events who have the lowest ratings. Since your body needs time to recover from the energy being released, limit yourself to forgiving ten (10) memories per day.

Next, say The Forgiveness Mantra for each one of the memories.

After you finish, immediately write down what emotion you feel next to the name.

If it's a negative one, then stand up and shake your body. Walk around the room. Then go back to the mantra, but this time just forgive the energy only. Return again when you feel ready to try again with this person/situation/event.

Be kind to yourself!

This is a marathon, not a sprint.

I suggest that you do this exercise every night before you go to bed. Please remember to not do more than ten (10) at a time because your body needs time to clear the energy and recover!

If you wish to download this workbook, then please visit my website at www.KatharineGiovanni.com.

Forgiveness Worksheet #1

List the names of the painful memories (people/ places/ events/ things) you would like to forgive. Once this page is filled with names, assign a rating next to each memory from one (1) to ten (10) with ten (10) being the most painful of the bunch.

Also, you might have multiple number ones (1s), or multiple number sevens (7s). It's all good.

Write as many painful memories as you like. I always start with the least painful ones first and work my up to the most painful memories.

Remember, you can forgive anything! People, places, situations, events, dates… anything goes.

Today's Date: _____

Rating	Name

Have more? Write them here. You can also grab a pad of paper and a pen to write down more.

Rating	Name

Forgiveness Worksheet #2

Using the list you created on the previous pages, write down the first ten (10) names you assigned numbers between 1 to 3.

Now say the mantra below your list. Afterwards, write down any emotion(s) you're feeling next to the name.

If the emotion is positive, then check the box next to the name!

If the emotion is negative, then stand up and shake your body for a bit. Walk around the room. Then come back and this time only forgive the energy. Not the name. Just the energy. Then go on to the next name on your list. You can return tomorrow and try to forgive that memory again.

Once you've done the first group, wait 24 hours and then take a brand-new worksheet and find the memories with ratings between four (4) and seven (7).

You get the idea! Once finished with group 2, then you wait 24 hours (or more if you like) and move onto group 3... the people/places/events you gave numbers eight (8) to ten (10) – these are the most painful ones.. Be kind to yourself as some of these might take some time to do.

If you need more worksheets, please visit my website at www.KatharineGiovanni.com

Memories Rated one (1) to three (3)

	Name	Emotion(s)

Start with the first name. Put your hand on your heart, and say the following

- I completely forgive <person/place/event.
- I completely forgive the energy around them/it.
- I completely forgive myself.
- I completely forgive the energy around me.
- I completely forgive the energy around the situation between us.
- Thank you.

NOTES

Did you remember something after you said the mantra? Feel/See/Know/Hear something?

Write it down here so you can refer back to it later.

```


```

Forgiveness Worksheet #3

Memories rated four (4) to six (6)

	Name	Emotion(s)

- I completely forgive <person/place/event.
- I completely forgive the energy around them/it.
- I completely forgive myself.
- I completely forgive the energy around me.
- I completely forgive the energy around the situation between us.
- Thank you.

NOTES

Did you remember something after you said the mantra? Feel/See/Know/Hear something?

Write it down here so you can refer back to it later.

Forgiveness Worksheet #4

Memories rated seven (7) to ten (10)

	Name	Emotion(s)

- I completely forgive <person/place/event.
- I completely forgive the energy around them/it.
- I completely forgive myself.
- I completely forgive the energy around me.
- I completely forgive the energy around the situation between us.
- Thank you.

NOTES

Did you remember something after you said the mantra? Feel/See/Know/Hear something?

Write it down here so you can refer back to it later.

Resources/Bibliography

For more information on how to book a private session with Katharine, please visit www.GuidedTalk.com, or visit her corporate website at www.KatharineGiovanni.com.

To book a session with Dr. Katie Nall, Ph.D., please visit www.GuidedTalk.com, or her corporate website at www.nalledgeco.com.

About the Author

Katharine is a three-time award-winning best-selling author of twelve books, speaker/trainer, mentor, and intuitive advisor. She is recognized as the pioneer who founded the independent concierge industry, leading the first association for independent concierges for over two decades before retiring in March 2023.

Throughout her career, Katharine has trained countless concierge and front-line staff, and her clients are among the industry's most successful. She has been featured in various prestigious media outlets, including ABC News Nightline, CBS News, Good Morning America, Forbes, The New York Times, and The Wall Street Journal to name a few.

Katharine, a proud breast cancer survivor, was raised in New York City, holds a B.A. from Lake Forest College, and currently resides in North Carolina. To learn more about her, visit www.KatharineGiovanni.com or www.guidedtalk.com.

SOURCES

https://psychology.fandom.com/wiki/Religious_views_of_forgiveness

https://greatergood.berkeley.edu/topic/forgiveness/definition

https://thelawofattraction.com/

https://www.healthshots.com/mind/mental-health/shake-your-body-to-shoo-away-the-stress-suggests-expert/

https://www.healthline.com/health/mental-health/can-shaking-your-body-heal-stress-and-trauma#Can-shaking-help-with-stress?

https://www.orgoneenergy.org/blogs/news/types-of-spiritual-energy

https://teacupsandlipsticks.com/3-ways-to-raise-the-vibrations-of-your-water/

https://globalnews.ca/news/4217594/bully-a-plant-ikea/

https://www.nccih.nih.gov/health/reiki

https://www.cbsnews.com/news/health-care-debt-40-percent-us-adults/

Printed in the USA
CPSIA information can be obtained
at www.ICGtesting.com
CBHW061104171223
2718CB00008B/792